A Gathering of Angels

Edited by Peter Eyvindson

BROKEN
WINGS
MISSIONS
INC.

Printed and Bound in Canada
1ˢᵗ printing 2003

National Library of Canada Cataloguing in Publication

A Gathering of Angels / Peter Eyvindson, Editor

Prayers written and illustrated by children from St. Joseph's Home for Boys,
Wings of Hope and Trinity House in Haiti

ISBN 0-9684918-1-2

1. Christian Children—Prayer—Books and Devotions—English
2. Children's Writings—Haitian
3. Children's Art—Haiti   I. Eyvindson, Peter

BV265.G368 2003   242'.82   C2003-900112-1

To receive additional copies of
this book, please contact:

BROKEN WINGS MISSIONS INC.
Box 51
Clavet, SK Canada
S0K 0Y0

Jesus, I don't see You but
I do believe in You.
I know You see me and that You love me.

Closini (9)

Glorious God, thank you for filling my life with so much color.
Thank you for teaching me to add to the beauty of life
by developing my talents.
Help me express my love for You by being creative.
Send angels of art to inspire me.

Draw within my heart a picture of Your love for me.
I will draw on canvas pictures of my love for You.

Dear God, I am one of Your works of art.
Help me to see Your hand at work in my life.
Help me recognize Your work in others, too.
Help me remember to compliment them because
when I tell others about the beauty I see in them and their work,
I am also praising and honoring Your beauty.

Dear God, You deserve the very best.
I want to live my life in the best way I can.
I want the angels of heaven to see You in me.
I want them to help me see as You see.
I want them to help me love as You love.

Julner (20)

Dear God,
Please send Your angels out to the streets.

There are many
        sad people,
                and hurt people,
                        and sick people who need You.
Help them!

Some are washing cars,
Some are shining shoes,
Some are stealing cars and going to jail.
Some are hurting others and breaking bones.
Some need to go to the hospital.

Please God, send more angels out to the streets to help these people.

Ralph (9)

God, please!

Bless the cook so that the food doesn't burn
and everything tastes good.

Thank you for good smells
and the fun of working with others.

I help chop the bell peppers and onions.

I peel carrots and potatoes.

I sweep the kitchen floor and help wash pots and pans.

I don't really like washing the pots and pans
But the cook gives us treats for helping.

So, dear God,
Help me to be a good cooking angel.

Ralph (9)

Creator God, You have done a good job
Of making a beautiful world.
Help us keep this world beautiful.
When we have jobs to do, help us do our best.
Help us not be lazy.

Dear God, I pray for all people
Who use their lives to make
This world more beautiful.
I pray for people who paint
        and carve wood
                and cook good food.

Inspire them and protect them.
Give them happy hearts so that
Their art will make others happy.
Give them the money they need
To buy paint and wood and food.

Fignole (9)

God of life,
You help me lift up my feet and dance.
You send Your angels to give me joy.
I hear Your voice in the drum beat.
My body thanks You with its dance.

Give me the energy I need to dance my best.
When I dance, I am happy.
I smile.
When I dance, I know You dance with me.

Dear God,
Please bless my dance teacher.
Bless those who dance next to me.
Help those who do not dance learn to dance,
Even if it is only with their hearts.

Jeff (13)

Great God, I like to dance.
When I think of the angels in heaven I see them dancing
Because they are happy to be with You.

Sometimes I dance with my friends.

Sometimes I dance alone.

Sometimes I dance in front of people from other countries.
They clap their hands and are happy.
I like making people happy.

Sometimes I dance with children in wheelchairs and they laugh with joy.

Once I danced for some children in prison.
It was sad to see them there, but they were happy to see me dance.

God, thank you for sending some of Your angels to help me dance.
Thank you for teaching me to dance.

When I live with You in heaven, I will be one of Your dancing angels.

Patrick (12)

Creator God,
You have done a good job of making a beautiful world.

Help us keep this world beautiful.

When we have jobs to do,
Help us do our best.

Help us not be lazy.

Roni (15)

Jesus did You ever get into trouble?
Were You ever sad?

Sometimes I get into trouble and then I have to sit in a chair.

Sometimes when I am in that chair, I think about You.

Sometimes I fall asleep.

I don't like getting into trouble.

Can You help me so I don't have to sit in that chair.

You know I am a good person.
Please, show me how to be obedient and kind.
When I want to fight with someone or tease someone
Help me to be nice to them instead.

It isn't easy doing the right thing.
Was it easy for You?

Jesus, help me do what is right
So I can go out and play with my friends
and

STAY OUT OF THAT CHAIR!

Jeff (13)

Father!

Please listen to my prayer.

> Children are hungry.
> Children are sad and alone.
> Children are crying.
> Children are scared.

Send them angels of joy and encouragement.
Send them angels to protect them from harm.

But, Father
Where are Your angels of mercy?
Are they sitting in their comfortable clouds
When children need Your help?

Tell those angels there is work to do!

Send Your angels to tell the children that You hear their prayers.

Gayly (12)

God,
Thank you for the clothes that You give me.
Thank you for sending someone to wash the clothes.
Thank you for helping me find my clothes on the clothesline once they are dry.
Thank you for bright colors and new buttons.
Thank you for socks that match.

Closiny (9)

Good God, I praise You for giving me strength to live my life.
I praise You for making my heart happy and my body healthy.
I praise You for giving us electricity so I can listen to music.
I praise You for giving me friends.
I praise You for cold water on hot days.
I praise You for letting me know You and love You.

Franco (17)

Dear God, let me hear Your voice. Let me know that You are with me.
You are my hope. You are my happiness.
I call out to You with trust. Please hear me.

Although I don't hear Your voice,
I do feel You are with me,
Communicating in the language of the angels.

You have placed people in my life who speak to me of You.
There are people who are Your voice of encouragement.
Others communicate Your love through their actions.

Through others I have come to know that You are with me.
I don't hear You with my ears.
I hear You with my eyes and my heart.

Help me keep my eyes and my heart attentive to Your Word.

Alcindor (25)

Jesus, my life is filled with angels of love.

They sing to me,
      They laugh with me,
            They comfort me,
                  They encourage me!

The angels of love enliven me and remind me that You want me to be an angel of love too!

Sometimes I look at my failings and I don't feel anything like an angel. Then,
You search me out in the darkness.
You bring me light.
You forgive me and help me see my angel wings again!

Jesus, help me be an angel of Your love.
Touch my heart with generosity so that I will share Your love with everyone in my life.
Fill my mind with wisdom so that I can tell the truth about You to others with clarity.

It is my sincere desire
To love You,
To praise You, and
To serve You in thought, word and deed.

Keep me on the right road,
      The road of the angels,
            The road that will lead me home to You!

Choupy (18)

Dear Jesus,

I like meeting new people.
I like all the people that spend time with me.
When I am with happy people, I am happy.
Jesus, help me be a happy person so that other people will be happy to be with me, like they are happy to be with You.

Ralph (9)

Good God, thank you for my life and good health.
Thank you for the people who come to visit.
Thank you for songs and flowers and hugs.

Closiny (9)

Dear God,

Thank you for all the people you have put in my life to help me.
I have friends from different countries.

We pray together.

We play together.

We laugh together.

We don't speak the same language
But we still understand each other because we have the same heart.

Help me not be afraid to make friends with people because they are different from me.

Help me remember that we are all one family.

Lafrance (17)

Creator God,
The world I live in is a beautiful place.

Thank you for the trees and all the good fruit they give us.
　　　Mangoes,
　　　　　　Bananas, Pineapples.
　　　　　　　　Coconuts and Papayas.
Pineapples are my favorites.

Thank you for the beautiful flowers.
I like their colors and the way they smell.
I like giving flowers to people and seeing how those flowers make people smile.

Thank you for the ocean and the fun I have playing in the cool water.

Thank you for the fish. There are so many different kinds.
I like fish to eat with rice and red beans and tomatoes.

Thank you for music: the music of birds and the music of people.

I like to make music on the drums.
I like to sing.
I like to dance.

I like living in this beautiful world You created.

What kind of world have You created in heaven?

I know it will be a beautiful place because I know You love me.

I love You too!

Fignole (9)

Photo Credit: Renee Dietrich

Lucson, Julner and Walnes dedicate the illustrations for this book to their mentor and teacher, Ralph Allen.

Ralph Allen, born in Haiti in 1952, began his studies in Port au Prince before receiving a scholarship in 1971 to study at the National Academy School of Fine Arts in New York.

Returning to Haiti in 1976, his art has demonstrated a passion for the markets of the poorer areas of Port au Prince.

His seriousness, his ardor for his work and his openness with his young students has made him a professor without equal.

Thank you, Ralph Allen.

Photo Credit: Renee Dietrich